The Phoenix Living Poets

THAT SINGING MESH

Poets Published in

The Phoenix Living Poets Series

*

JAMES AITCHISON
GEORGE MACKAY BROWN · MICHAEL BURN
PHILIP CALLOW · JOHN COTTON
GLORIA EVANS DAVIES
PATRIC DICKINSON
D.J. ENRIGHT
JOHN FULLER
J.C. HALL · MOLLY HOLDEN
P.J. KAVANAGH
CHRISTOPHER LEVENSON
EDWARD LOWBURY · NORMAN MacCAIG
DIANA McLOGHLEN
JAMES MERRILL
LESLIE NORRIS · RICHARD OUTRAM
RODNEY PYBUS
ADRIENNE RICH · ANNE SEXTON · JON SILKIN
JON STALLWORTHY
EDWARD STOREY · TERENCE TILLER

THAT SINGING MESH

and Other Poems

By

TERENCE TILLER

CHATTO AND WINDUS

THE HOGARTH PRESS

1979

Published by
Chatto & Windus Ltd
with The Hogarth Press Ltd
40 William IV Street
London WC2N 4DF

*

Clarke, Irwin & Co. Ltd
Toronto

British Library Cataloguing in Publication Data
Tiller, Terence
That singing mesh. – (Phoenix living poets)
I. Title II. Series
821'.9'12 PR6039.152T/

ISBN 0-7011-2409-1

Printed in Great Britain by
Redwood Burn Limited
Trowbridge and Esher

CONTENTS

Doubt you to whom my Muse these notes entendeth?

(Sir Philip Sidney: *Astrophel and Stella*)

△

FOREWORD

Many of the poems in this book have been broadcast in Radio Three, or in its precursor, the Third Programme. None is recent, a number of them ante-dating even those in my previous collection. As the title-poem suggests, however, they are the last that I shall write (excluding translations and perhaps light verse), and the last (apart from those) that I wish to be published. I should like this to be taken as an earnest plea to friends who may possess poems of mine, in typescript or manuscript, other than these printed here: destroy them, as I have destroyed my own copies.

Epic and dramatic poems are not often suspected of being autobiographical; and I do not see why these mostly lyrical poems, either, should come under that suspicion.

Short notes upon the more difficult poems will be found at the end of the book. Annotated poems are marked with an asterisk against the title.

T.T.

MOCKING THE WIND

She found my cousin mop-faced as a gargoyle,
his young spine Quasimodo'd against summer:
          "Careful!", his mother told him.
"You'll have to stay like that if the wind changes."

I will stand upright in your steady shining,
wear for you nothing but my bridegroom-smile:
          oh love, I know already
the grey-glass moment when the wind must change.

THE TRAP

Mandarins thought that any five-doored room
would call a ghost; or many; and they built
no such a gin unless they knew for whom
(nets random-cast may catch us our own guilt,
or a sea-monster. Only fool or mage
blindly constructs what is both lure and cage).

My pentacle of senses, it well knows,
and not with terror, is inhabited:
from door to door the single spectre goes,
finding no issue, because not yet dead.

It was not I who pierced the walls, or locked
(inside or out?) the spells that brought me her
—that brought her me: for the design is mocked;
the seeming prison is the prisoner.

A WASTE OF SHAME

Let it be thought, at least, that I can read
with open lids: a body is not braille.
Yes, give the blind their flower-vase, and feed
two senses: but—are flowers dark, or pale?
Let sensuous alabaster lead the hand
through joy: but—how shall fingers pierce the veil
of that uncolour of night's eyeless land?
Its glory, not a curtain, clothed the Grail.

I have kept roses pressed within a book,
memorial gifts: what could they do but die?
That is a love at which one does not look.
And, when the love itself was sour and dry,
have let them burn, a symbol I mistook,
that should have once made happy lip and eye.

CHRISTMAS AND EPIPHANY

The visible night is tall and overstarred;
cold like a ringing glass, the hound-fang wind,
its tower of echoes: Christmas; and the cord
of the old year drawn tight (my hungering hand
roving along it, rediscovering
airs first awakened in it by your touch,
then given me). And do you know how much
will shudder at the breaking of that string?

Withdraw your senses from that outward night:
the true (ten-fingered on my calendar,
ten-petalled, doubly-bloomed, within my heart)
is hidden—all that have been ours, and are,
in one calm darkness; you its warmth of wheat,
its threefold gift, its one prophetic star.

IN ABSENTIA

Flaws in the burning-glass—the heart perhaps
left empty, or a limbus wounded, or
the arc imperfect—and its virtues lapse:
its gathered light achieves a point no more,
only a wan aureola, shadow-sun.
And I have seen a watch (the escapement wried)
in helpless fever all-but-invisibly run
past any meaning, till the spiral died.

Who is the lens your presence must perfect;
and, like the glass in darkness, have no power
without your sun to focus and reflect?
Who is the watch whose motion you must keep?
A day or death can else fill every hour
with time amok, or with all springs asleep.

SEVERANCE

Dante: *Inferno*, Canto 34

Heaven wears deep beyond Satanic ice,
and partings wider than in triple jaws:
union obeys its own bedazzling laws,
shields of the flower-hive of Paradise.
Heaven holds many that see only one
(as we two might); nor can their Gloria pause
while multiplicit radiance lives on.
What harps will sour, though, if the fire withdraws!

But glaciered rocks demand no anodyne.
Ice and aurora! When the sun-day bleeds
like a cut flower, and the lights are down
to lair of octopus, to bed-crabs' roads;
when star and pestilence awake at noon:
where is your gift? All deeps are solitudes.

INTERCALATION

Between the Old Year and the New there lay,
uncalendared, a time of amnesty:
one hundred one score hours; nor any day
asking account of guilt or secrecy.
These, lacking month and ordinal, became
their own white dominoes against sin or shame.

When change of season spooled the minutes back,
an hour became a ghost, then lived again.
Where was its place upon the almanac?
What gift was real in it, or what stain?
Better: the clock moved forwards, and a space
was opened lacking all of ill or grace.

A medicine against whatever ails!
Then let reluctance or disgust be torn
out of your calendar: the love avails,
the uncorruption dies or is not born:
if harm were meant, harm could not clutch or live
in the intercalation you might give.

TERRA INCOGNITA

Old sailors making landfall (but the tide
unruly and the wind uncertain) boast,
in their home port, of beauties undescried.
Fog had kept modest all that skirted coast;
no matter, legends knew the hinterland:
all was a cradle of lotos, flower or fruit;
islanders gentle, jewels many, and
the strongest storm as lulling as a flute.

Or so they say; and so the maps are made.
Valleys and orchards, gardens and springs, are guessed;
even the shape, that never was surveyed,
they make what symbol satisfies them best.
Only—one thrust of conscience?—at the centre
their lying falters, their inventions lapse:
these are the woods not even thought might enter.
There are white spaces on the best of maps.

Legends are built of longing: my own ship,
wind-racked and wary, hovers off the shore
of your enshrouded island; hand and lip
know little of that Eden, guess the more;
eyes (fox-hair, elf-rose, firm and delicate wand)
map all your beauty in the veils' despite
—shine for the apples and the flowers beyond;
but fall before your secrecies of white.

THE MARBLE CURTAINS

Not the true secrecies of cups or flowers,
soft arrowheads, or garden of the fox,
nor slender paths of silk to climb like lutes;
they are still yours; a dream to call them ours:
sightless the jewels, folded the pale flocks,
arcane the orchards and their guarded fruits.

Not the true secrecies. But flesh and word
have borne a moth-call through the lilac air,
or ghost of wings, or grass-breath of a phrase
(conjectures of the tree-invisible bird)
naming by absence what is darkly there.
The nymph within the marble knew such ways:

imaging all no less denying all,
she was the mover of the shaping hand,
the life that waited on Pygmalion's lip.
Unreal till the useless fragments fall,
beauty is waiting to be sunlit, and
to ride your alabaster like a ship.

STAGE DIRECTIONS *

Now let your stage lie bare, the lights contract;
we know the masquers are not far away:
there is a curtain for the final act.

If we have kept the dual text intact,
no change of scene imports, and no delay:
now let your stage lie bare, the lights contract.

The cast uneasy, timing inexact?
That comfort is not least by which we say
"There is a curtain for the final act".

The songs are fiction, but the plot is fact;
there is a past that we must not betray.
Now let your stage lie bare, the lights contract.

Let the two eponyms alone compact
exchange of parts: the end is sure as they
—there is a curtain for the final act.

Oh living theatre that I have lacked,
if not between your wings, where shall I play?
Now let your stage lie bare, the lights contract:
there is a curtain for the final act.

NEED-FIRES *

The most of pain is greater than its need;
but who shall draw the colours from the glass
until the firing becomes death indeed?

To snatch reluctant wings is baby greed
(lust is a foundry that unfuses brass):
the most of pain is greater than its need.

Love is the fruit on which the wasp will feed,
the adder haunting clean and scented grass
until the firing becomes death indeed.

Noosed within kisses that made neither bleed,
lover and victim speak the same *Alas*:
the most of pain is greater than its need.

The born-too-early learns a bitter creed,
all rituals and sacraments must pass
until the firing becomes death indeed.

No harvest crowns the burning of the seed
that strains and parches in the dried morass:
the most of pain is greater than its need
—until the firing becomes death indeed.

LIMITS *

What if the winches coil-up all the rope,
the tall man's toes and fingers riding on
the drums; he, raised, a secretary's M
above the rack-bed—twanged, a fiddle E?
This pain, at this point, asks a substitute.

How often lovers dream their curve is closed:
what if their love lacks focus—if their functions
produce hyperbolae? Or the least variable
be their divisor (zero alone gives aleph)
and the failed asymptote aspire for ever?

Less happy than the recusant, they lie
unbound indeed, yet never to know limits
but those of their too-mortal graph; the pain
eased by no pawl-slip, ended by no burning,
because no substitute is possible.

DEATH BY WATER *

Lovers will vaunt the pains of Lawrence, threaten
a death to out-flame Latimer, the sky
one fog and thunder from their throes: they lie.
Their fires are tame and captive, soon forgotten
when the cold flesh learns comfort, souls are dry.

Air is not lighter than the vows it carries,
for the untortured living tongue vibrates
as butterfly as they: one lie creates
the Venus-trap, the words that vulcan Ares,
the folding-out of horn or ivory gates.

Gatepost or stake or tree is earth-embedded;
the lust of pyres, the airy poem, yields
to the slow seeding of the worm-bred fields.
Worm in the blood, and of the blood, be guided:
dreams and the ardent boast are tinsel shields.

The death is in the deep: the mateless ocean,
the river's nunnery, the brooding well—
Phlebas, Ophelia, Truth. O asphodel,
witness how many, drunk upon compassion,
died in the dew of one white mercy-bell.

BLESSING

. . .the continual dew of Thy blessing. . .
(The Book of Common Prayer)

Not only for the small blind eyes of dew,
though ever-waking, nor the rainbow's promise,
although a giant image of those waters;
nor the uncovenanted lights that wash
dark and the day in spectra, though unbounded:
not thankfulness for these alone, by sight
or symbol; but for laws that gave us them.

All the great shining of so many mercies
impurely reaches us through prism and lens
of angel-flesh or blood-of-clouds or sky-dust:
blessing is mediate, screened by elements,
flying the lanes of sense, empowered by sense:
if light is pure, it is invisible
(the dark of God): light is the eye that sees.

Blessing is mediate, even that of love:
our thicker flesh, our living dust, our white
and crimson distillations, are the world
by which it acts, unguessed without them; love
enthroned in secrecy, but love which is
a peacock wheel of stars, a moon, a morning,
a rainbow peace, and a continual dew.

PEACOCK NIGHT

Therefore the black fan, white-and-prism-eyed,
was opened, and that emblematic bird
erected over us the rest of pride.

Not in displaying darkness to be heard,
the witch-cry of his prophecy: he kept
his bleak—our amorous—council, and his word.

And so the lovers and the augur slept,
three lulling three with breath and with nó fear;
and it was only light that Argus wept.

Never awaken for the dream you hear
from his upraised his mantic throat: endure
whatever nights enfold each other: dear,

the auspice of the peacock is unsure.

THE FUGUE OF POEMS *

Why, then, the lines of astral celebration
—sky colour, calendar and zodiac,
narrowing to the poem's needle-eye;
arrow intention bridewell-broadening
into the poem's air and mapless nation
escapeless as the prisoner's looking-back
or voluntary cell-mouse?
There is "why"
even within the beds' quadruple wing
where to this dark the exceeding lovers lie.

He who has mastered manuals—flesh or speaking
be they—and the false ivory of rhyme,
knowing the spectral escalade of key,
forgoing fugue, holding most answers back
but the last unison or suspension breaking
tension upon the common chord, in time:
one such will know all disciplines in me.
Thus my auroras, drowning white and black;
sought harmonies I hear, but feel and see.

READING A SCORE *

They who by February mist, by March
blue-gashing in the cold new-nippled boughs,
loved under day or under the dark brows
of sheetless night; poised their brief-straining arch
at Now or Maybe-never: by Easter grace
awhile were given time, and Time, and place.

Closed on each other's flesh as flowers close
upon themselves, how should they sense or care
when the black moth their paraclete spread there
a sparked eclipse of wings on thorn and rose?
Fires have more colour, overshaded; peace
more purity when song and cradle cease.

But instruments, as well as echoes, die?
Still, in the quiet of the fugue that failed
(the stops immovable, a wolf that wailed
the *vox humana* down, the couplers wry,
the swell unanswering), upon the score
entry and answer sang as theretofore.

So many modes in which to fail and fear!
Though all he planned as music be unplayed,
all given time be lost, all fire mislaid,
they read the printed chords they cannot hear,
move with their thought the unsounding keys, and light
with silent verse the lamps of Easter night.

SYNAESTHESIA

Nipple to emerald, rose to mercaptan, hell
to the Aurora's curtains: and how far
from Re to Mi? Your sex to Satan's fell,
dew by the glow-worm to the dying star,
and Beatrice to Lilith: count the kinds,
if they are there for counting. But I see
feathers and farms blown by ill-matching winds:
nothing can differ except by degree.

Give rabies to the rose, castrate the gem,
drink the bright vacuum, burn out of scale,
open your thighs to spectra; closing them,
shut-out the beetle, snuff the linking Grail:
the paradox of species will not stand.
So, naming love or Love—take Paul or Sade
for the pure A—only the staircase hand
can teach our strings how harmonies are made.

Lock-in the rabid weasel with your flowers,
and they will breed; give me the light, and I
will make the stone a soft consent of hours:
the deepest images are those that lie.
Change as you may, the meanings can but rhyme.
How shall a bezel bite one out of key?
From animal to chord, from flesh to time,
nothing can differ except by degree.

TRIPTYCHS *

I: *Aspects of Barbara*

That flower-born by whom the lost forgive,
Blodeuwedd, knows this other name as hers.
Thrice-universal, thrice-affirmative

(alone, so being), and by no demurs
eluctible, she strings their lyre upon
the Delphic tripos of the sophisters,

returning reason for their worship: gone,
as Barbara, the lunar flesh they kissed –
grown mad as though from ivy – and the wan

sky-felspar of her bridal wine, her mist
of panic hope: she cures their drunkenness
by the clear morning of the amethyst.

The lovers' planet, bourne of their excess,
conclusion of their premisses (the Maid
and Thief) is light they only half-possess:

buds are unfolded that our fires invade,
but vanish soon from their illusive sun;
so spirits whom she wakes are early laid

in ash of hoarfrost, all their seed undone.
Let birds then be her only avatars:
Blodeuwedd's flowers winter one by one;

Barbara's triptych is blasphemed by scars
cat-lusted on it; and the cannibal
mare, the mad sow, were banished from our stars.

But, in the tundras of our after-fall,
spare us memorial doves' wind-opalling;
spare us the cranes that will destroy us all

if they return among the mimes of Spring;
spare us the night and rapture of the owl,
Cassandra's cry upon her desolate wing.

These are the flesh that she inhabits, fowl
of her emblem: *every tenderness*
lapses in danger and the sibyl's cowl;

every death foretold is a caress;
oh Barbara, by whom the lost forgive,
love ends in love and its devouring dress.

II: *Figure One*

Barbara Celarent Darii Ferio...

Continually then to shroud from us
their Persian cruelties in the forms of reason—
moods of sweet order, figures perspicuous

as triangles—they ravished our long prison
with bannered sieges of embroidered laws
dove-purring though draconic; false horizon

of amative arras. While their knives and saws
opened harems of wounds in us, their hammers
trod vineyards on our flesh, they sang the cause

in wry faburden syllogism, drummers
to their own lullaby. We were allayed,
oh truly, by such furbishers and psalmers.

All miracles are born from love (they said);
are not your agonies a preternature?
It is by love that now you are dismayed.

Vagitus fails in joy that begs a future;
dear chronicles dress bright with almanacs;
none of your spectra was a living creature.

From pride alone a man believes he lacks;
the wildfires of your pain are greed and searching;
it is vainglory chafes at screws and racks.

Charity springs beneath no miser's watching;
in its degree, the scourge is merciful;
ferio!, *then: I lash for your enriching. . .*

Are we less blind for lying in that school,
glossing the dangerous moods of Media,
forgoing our allies from their twisted rule,

than surely alone on the sand (andabata
tensing for net-man), masked in one triad, thus:
"all", "all", and A "All": the naked Barbara?

III. *The Second Figure*

Cesare Camestres Festino Baroco. . .

Say she had come among us a mystery—
unfound in charvering and unapt for chivving,
by Occam blade or Hampton patency:

could we have bent her to our beat of living?
How little we, though, understood what swung
our impassioned pendulum, or our forgiving

bell of good reason with its golden tongue!
We should have known her (if she took our schooling)
older than lust itself; and no less young.

She did not come unknown to our befooling,
nor daisy-thighed, nor meaning us any shame:
but she and all her sisters, overruling

our diffident hatch, fine-drew the mating-game
to Lilith-meshes of perpetual checks.
Thus, echo-name by Malabranca name,

they hung the Nine of Primes about our necks:
a sigil in the place of lauds; the orders
of reasoned service in the vast of sex.

None, in their sweet enclave, can woo his warders;
unconsummated love must kiss the bars:
no captive princes *are within these borders.*

Virginal scars meet *with placental scars;*
the sisters were Palladian of bearing:
they went in tunics, not in scapulars.

Say she had come among us never caring
for the Frome answer (bulldyke, philosopher,
pouf, or anaesthetist, or the outstaring

clergy)? *I hasten* (could we have hastened her?);
no new is good new; hells may be justly novel,
but may be neither for nor on the spur.

Yet she made all, in this Baroque *sub-hovel*
of shadow-life, except the hoping part—
and, but for that, what need have we to grovel?

We cannot leave her: it is she we chart
in lust-with-reason's ill geology.
But love is the huge nifė at her heart.

WITH THE GIFT OF SPRING FLOWERS

You my pavilion and my power,
by whom to sleep and wake and not forget,
we cast the seed of every flower
when your and my uncovered knowledge met:
in token of that hour,
the petals of sharp spring are valent yet.

As cold and bitter as the wine
of winter graves, and red as childhood grief,
yours be the calyces; and mine,
the symbol of the scabbards of green leaf:
true neither way, but sign
against the superstition of the thief.

Let symbols go by opposites,
like dreams, and all the dancing-maze of joy
misname itself; and thus the writs
our years may draft against us shall destroy
only the lie and its
pale worm or virus at their dark employ.

BIRTHDAY SONG

The day is not for our delight,
nor is the light what we believe;
under the lampless eaves of night,
blindly for wonder at her white,
the lover in his living sleeve
is giving more, and will receive,
than in the naked land of sight.

But many be your nights and days,
a gallery of praise and peace:
time will release, and spring will raise,
that prisoned king, who by the ways
of risen stars will know increase
until the dance the dancer cease
and the still trance of music stays.

A SONG IN G-SHARP MINOR

In my beginning is my end. . . (*East Coker*)
Teach us to care and not to care (*Ash Wednesday*)

Give me the only answer
that hope and sense may know;
fetter the future dancer
and singer and entrancer:
give me the only answer,
and let the garlands go.

Is care the end of caring,
desire the end of grief,
gay garment of my wearing?
Bartholomew, my fairing
is care, the end of caring,
the dry but golden leaf.

The lost are sure of winning
a Garden and a Gate;
the penny spins, and spinning
turns end into beginning;
the lost are sure of winning:
and if they win too late?

NICHT ZU ERNST

I have seen them scuttle, faces long as a fish,
drizzling dislike from their grey-paper-bag bodies,
maggoting joy and thought, styptic to flesh,
Lenten umbrellas, black-lint-hearted ladies:
but you, my pear, my birthday, my bright penny,
my window-box, my bird-of-paradise cloak,
you my aurora, you my bath of honey,
have driven them back into the wickerwork.

I have heard them talking, sour tin-whistle voices
like fingernails on slates, intending ill,
achieving vanity and their own disgraces;
their poison-spittle, though, slug-silvering all:
but you my wing, my guinea Roman Candle,
my double-century, my Book of Kells,
my Nobel Prize, my mink, my triple rondel,
have rung them silent with your platinum bells.

But, my blue-ribbon, my four-minute-mile,
my cherry-gold pagoda, my concerto,
my smuggled brandy-wine, my swallow-tail,
my Kohinoor, my phoenix, my del Sarto,
my Stradivarius, my New Atlantis,
how shall I wholly shut the door on them
who flood me like a Sorcerer's Apprentice,
and bar the bloom from the aspiring stem?

THREE POEMS FROM *DIAPASON* *

I: *Luna*

Honour to virgins! Of the elements, all
but five are lustful, and possessed; but these,
nobly inert, viewless, ethereal,

even in heat repel the valencies
of baser fabric (base because erect
with double gender). Such virginities,

the lunar hand of pearl of the elect,
gas-goddesses, are counted soon indeed:
what of those other vestals, to perfect

whose indivisible maidenheads there breed
no parent figures?—and from whose power descends
ipse alone? Like unpredictable seed,

they flower still where number itself extends:
other, and hybrid, rabble-integers reach
beyond themselves (Aleph begins, not ends):

these are as many, though; for each to each
—as facing mirrors double and recede—
must correspond. Not so the forms of speech:

honour to those for whom there are decreed
no proper mates, whom charts of rhyme reject.
For months of iron may be paired at need;

never the iceberg plinth, or insurrect
sistrum of wyvern dogma: silver keys
that open mirrored nothing, nor connect

with any ward. Here fertile numbers freeze
as well as primes: few that are cardinal;
most, that name place or that assign degrees.

And, all being virgin, honour to them all!

II. *Venus*
The Song of Solomon 2:5 (Authorised Version)

With flagons of what metal? In the bloom
of copper, transubstantiate wines must bleed
thin as the milk of garnets—knowing whom,

oh Cyprian, their shell is named for. Feed
on apples of what colour? On the bough
all gold and flame; but lusted for, untreed,

of bitter emerald. The lover now
eats without comfort, drinks and never slakes
—your goblets too turned-green. Oh Cyprian, how

flourish on fables when your power breaks?
—on paradox and horror and nightmare bride:
testes of toadstools, hag-sperm, hair of snakes,

or sweat of beetles? Yet your power died
from hope witheld: not like a dish let fall,
but like a priapism unsatisfied.

Rare in your transits, have you thought at all
by hidden sunlight your albedo wakes,
that riding past His face grows dark and small?—

all the long shining while the lover aches,
ends in a blemish on Apollo's brow?
Ancient your empire, narrow your mistakes,

but you have no more damsels to endow;
the hands that flattered once are hooked in greed;
the wells are poisoned, and the steeples bow.

Dry nipples are the grapes your kisses knead;
Hesperides, as withered as your womb,
upraise the maggot in the cups of seed:

rose, you are sour: let the sweet nightshade bloom.

III: *Sol*

How is it with you, around Helicon,
deserted poet? Are they to your mind,
these groves and streams, the Muses being gone?—

all but the lying Clio and the blind
Urania. Forget those golden wires
that no more shiver and spell within your vined

academy, nor kindle from your fires.
Apollo, neither prophet nor who sings,
poor little shrewmouse of abandoned choirs,

your vatic hymns gnawn into mutterings,
your topaz chariot in the deep and cone
of annular eclipse: the chords and springs

of the fine fountain are no more your own,
your dawning dwindled to a corposant,
and your new-pubic Daphne a dry crone.

After its nuptial flight, the fallen ant
walks tunnelled earth, has loved its last of wings:
thus with your aery horse; now he must pant

—gone in the wind, spavined and thrushed—on strings
twisted or shrunk: for shame to his dead sires,
a gelding, glandered. Ride him now? That brings

no more Aeolian madness in the gyres
of middle-aether, bird-and-blaze-entwined:
true laureates are mounted on entires.

God of the broken music, the dead rind
of manhood, have you wreaths to rest upon?
Bowman-avenger paled, oh light declined,

dark be your comfort around Helicon.

DOUZAINS

I: *Yeti*

Shake out your dragon streamers; autumn the snows
with balefire, link, or demon thurible;
strike-up the horrors of the horn and gong;
shiver my citadels with incantation;
and do all this in fear of me: with cause.

You have not seen me: pugs or slides, perhaps;
entrails and skins of the mouse-hare my food;
and you have heard me—or the blizzard?—crying
along the cols: but have not seen me. How
should I, your darkness made external, guilt
made flesh, old panic in my unman's mask,
submit myself a mirror to your hatred?

II: *Adam (i)*

As connoisseur of the impossible,
myself to choose and name the trees forbidden,
I would have nothing in this garden altered.
A dead leaf to be pruned (or the whole suffers),
a live to bend away (and the fruit ripens);
a cherishing (eidolon of possession);
even a plaque (as: *Malus Caritatis*):
these I permit. But *o dilecta mea*,
the spoiling foxes bite at apples also;
I cannot guard against their hungering.
How to be sure (no mirrors in the leaves)
the mask that *I* present you is not vulpine?

III: *Adam (ii)*

Bird in my stony garden, single flower,
dove I shall die of, rose be ruined by,
do I avenge already my unmaking?

Touches and words that spelt-out *love*: to you
are these a braille that ends in pain or pity,
a vexing as from fever-bird or mynah?

Knowing you native to the march of sadness,
I could forgive myself in your forgiving,
were this vast hand of shadow not my own
that clutches me.
                                        Sweet plumage I shall never
silken again, wine-petals not breathe-in,
commend my ashes to your patroness.

IV: *Parentheses*

I am not ready for the autumn (weather,
be faithful to this fallacy; St. Luke,
you shall see burned a yard of maiden wax).
But calendar and falling leaf and glass
wear the one image—happy enough did all
affections fade in the same season: how
if weathered stubble yearns for daffodils?

Turn, then, this planet penguin-over-walrus:
australe speculum. Or (since who has magic?)
cross-fold the star-map to a fair projection,
sowing the photograph and not the field,
peruking soon-bald almanacs with poems.

V: *Autumn*

Fifteen, I needed no recipient
for amorous poems, nor a real object:
at most the briefly-and-far-seen beauty of strangers,
or some green Lilith only a new-learnt body.
The empty canvas and the unfleshed air
I limned and featured by the power and wish.

Fifty, the wish and power dislocated,
my portrait-gallery closed unlit, and poems
torn out of me like mandrakes: oh, the aurora
suckled in vain, is very thin and cold;
I need the cottage of the flesh, its lamplight,
its warmth of little walls, and supper waiting.

VI: *October*

Do not, among the foxed autumnal trees,
wish for the lamb and hare, the parrot-green:
plays are as proud in tarnished theatres
as in the fancy's gilt and jewel-fires.
Too manifold the dancing bells of March;
I beat the steady music of the sparse
ungardens of October. Love *him-real*,
in his chrysanthemum and rowan years,
that winter must inherit, and the ice.

Oh let him understand his shortening light
is yet sufficient for the ends of peace;
his cold-roofed evening, cradle to your sleep.

VII: *Last Supper* *

Male spiders must not be too early slain. (W. Empson)

Your elder sister, with a swallow's flight
already in her fury, the willow-slayer,
suppered her king-deceiver upon flesh:
his last meal, human; psalm her, nightingale.

The paschal coven, breaking lamb for Lamb,
drinking the scattered lintel-blood, consuming
(as He consumed) the Man soon to be Fish,
could never eat again their present symbol.

I have spun poems out of time and flesh,
webs I would have you lie on; if I come
offering these, they also are my seed:
allow my love, then: sup not yet, Arachne.

VIII: *The Muse*

The true terrors of Muses—flesh that kills
by single contact; purpose unreadable
before the final revelation; mouth
by nature fastened upon *all*—not these
I think to learn from you. But even if these,
I gladly abandon guard: how else be sure
I see you in the full-moon's danger?
Yes,
that I have learned already; but not from you.
But not from you. Yet. Then I ask you this:
eating me, eat me gently; dismissing me,
dismiss me kindly; for I do not need
pain to confirm in me the nature of darkness.

IX: *Writing on Glass*

I grave in diamond upon looking-glasses
(across my own, my name; on yours, my poems).
The white script overlays our living features,
reads in their absence, holds till the mirror breaks.

Windows I dare not ruin with graffiti
—not my own, even; and *your* panes look outwards
wider and oftener. By this frosty weather,
from the cold sill I write on them in crystals;
how rarely from within, and then on breath.

Keep, love, the weather cold—giving me honour
that through the unvapoured looping path your vision
may yet be clearer than through shrouded glass.

X: *The Cheque-book*

Opening my account, I took their pamphlet
of twenty-four cheques all presentable
if I could earn or were I given; all
not limiting, yet, the powers of my credit.

On eight my writing was illegible;
one I forgot to sign, and one misdated;
one spoiled and threw away; too many squandered;
with four, perhaps, drew currency enough
to keep from starving; only two, I think,
were stolen and repudiated. One
was not presented.
                    Down to my last I come;
but, being overdrawn, how can I pay you?

XI: *Four Rooms*

First was a window: Xanadu and Y Brasil
beyond it, rainbow-real continents;
custom and old hope statured like the ant.

Second, a gift of boughs: being in secret
quieter than a doll's-house, happy as grass,
dark as the calling odours of the moth.

And third, a city gate thrown wide: the gentle
invader needing no destruction, trust
of the hearth and flesh disarming as the sunlight.

Fourth was an altar to the sound of bells:
an only two, untouched; but on that altar
custom and old hope staring, still alive.

XII: *Lazarus (i)*
(*Luke,* 16:19ff.)

Lazarus, fainting at the rich man's doorstep,
saw the delights that epicure commanded
(as: phoenix-breast, the tongues of paradise-birds,
kebab of Colchis flamed on dragons' quills,
the flesh of unicorns)—and saw great panniers
pouting with broken meats: what Dives cannot,
servant or beggar shall not, swallow-up.
But anger, no; and hatred, no; nor envy:
the pauper understood the prodigal—
that some wealth may be squandered but may not
be shared; the very crumbs acquiring voice
in protest against glory delegated.

XIII: *Lazarus (ii)*

I cannot wish the Dives from whose banquet
myself am jalousied, the parabolic
envy, despair, and flame: why *should* he feel them?
—or I attempt the Heights of Abraham?
He shall have all the water that he will,
after his human sacrament. For I,
crouched in the portico of the waste-panniers,
taking my comfort from the tongues of dogs,
reserve two prides he is not rich enough
to purchase: I can live in lack of all
he is fed with; and it is I who celebrate
(vicarious poet) *his* mere happiness.

XIV: *Errors*

Should have been window, have instead been prism:
love is a white beam; I have scattered it.

Should have unjewelled; but kept on my opals:
love is the clear skin; I wore necklaces.

Should have breathed air, but was amazed with perfume:
love is to live-by; I have made it strange.

You have breathed into me, and that air is pure:
my poems add the groin and offered incense.

I have had your sigil on my heart all night:
the gift has entered me as tender gold.

Oh my impossible and lovely glass,
I should be drunken, or give *you* pure water.

PICTORIAL CALENDAR *

i
Tapiola (Sibelius)

Castor fiber losing one chisel-tooth
dwines of the opposite whose dentine, rebutted
by no Pollux, grows giant and retorted:
a matchless liberty that seals the mouth.
Worse; for the bent continuing of that growth
returns into its origin: unmated,
now the skull-biting prodigal, self-reinserted,
enters his brain-sty and lodges there till death.
Love will bite stiffly, but you may feed and cry
while its twin gouges too; and will not die
from ivory obsession, its point being paired.
But, gnawing upon nothing, look about
for chance or strength to wrench the killer out:
breaking your mouth so that your life is spared.

ii
Oiseaux tristes (Ravel)

There have been birds, though, all the winter—parched
anxieties over the peaked rare fox, the acres
corrugated as roofs to ring-on. Mockers
or pleaders, living on luck or hate, they have searched
the hopeless, found the all-but-useless, weathered
the whittling sky, the ogham of their tracks
ollaved on snow. Bland airscape soon, and sex,
and all the bonewood parrot-fluffed and feathered.
And then what will they do? *Saynt Valentyn
that art ful hy on-lofte*, not for your sake
their Burke-lipped wooing in the procreant green,
their more than human heat, their parenthood:
change has not changed them, nor will suns unmake
the chill and mood of their ancestral blood.

iii
Egdon Heath (Holst)

A rock lay in the weather on useless land:
one grimace (of a self neither forced nor chosen)
without an echo; and one gesture, a hand
once-for-all clenched upon *This*—chronic and frozen
but not into pain or patience or joy; into holding.
Only the shape was insurrect, and screamed,
only the minerals tolerant of unmoulding.
Can a stone sleep? Never believe it dreamed.
What Throne, then, moving over the desolation,
breathing the scarves of mist, bleaching the sun,
printed this atony like a careless thief?
—that single instant grip of incarnation
leaving the rock awakened and undone,
pear-bruised-and-spurted, wrenched as a winter leaf?

iv
Bushes and Briars (Trad.)

The hard blue the cloud-herd Aeolian wind;
and the trees baby-bald, waving like mongols:
I know the month's mind: now through bushes and
through briars *(oh deciduous taiga-jungles!)*
the flex-life and the winter-torpid flesh
are to be sucked and burning forth be hunted.
The oldest way to suffer is to wish;
the cleverest loss is when the wish is granted;
Aeolian then sometimes I am uneasy:
acts will exceed, there will be too much sun
to shelter from, the breastless rose turn blowsy,
imaginës revisit one by one,
discorded limbs rebound to locks of time
unkept unkeyed unkempt, the lipping-game.

v
Le Réveille-matin (Couperin)

Well, but the clock at least was vigilant
—duenna-face, duenna-voice, with tongue
to wag the scandal of the seconds. Blent
caduceus-like together, lost among
their love, their bodies, and the lancet noon
beyond the curtains, time a Möbius tape,
they spared no senses to the chaperone
who threatened all: the cup was theirs to keep.
And tick by tick the clock was filling it;
honey and quinine drip with the same noise,
and who were they to wonder which was here
—their mutual tongues being what they tasted? Not
till the rim wept could they challenge her
who mixed her own secretion with the bees'.

vi
Les Noces (Stravinsky)

Under consent, intention, and with colour
of unchosen jewels—and the rite
of gathered flower-heads that kiss the culler,
the moving petals that are tilled by right.
Under delight, the auditor, the idle
autograph set firm in figures, ward
of the wet portico the rocking idol,
and the impasse where only space has warred.
Pattern of author of strait anguish; praise
of the eventual not found emotion
on which the answer not the question preys;
fish that are older than what ails them; ocean
that cannot fail and is not filled: unmanner
now unmade; rhyme in the making manner.

vii
Jardins sous la pluie (Debussy)
Der Gärtner (Wolf)

Let the twin ivies creep, antler you spiders,
over this white bough, on this web of sense;
there is nothing to be ravished that Invaders
Eponymous have not; captured, that pretence
if no more did not; king of the rosy adders,
built cobra-bolt, invest though your immense
for unseen empire of the covert riders:
summer's temptation and of Providence.
The fated standards flourish over sour
warrens of ant and worm, the sceptres dip
their sorcery to the baths of colder kaisers;
still, virtuous foxglove, yield that cordial flower
in the consensus of the parted lip:
open your lovely bite, my soft scissors.

viii
Daphnis and Chloe (Ravel)

In this high scrubland, wether-cropped, bleak-thistled,
ferment of bees and sun, cool-ribboned air
wafting wild apple: these two rested here,
over the tolerance of the sea; blue-castled
by their solitude; their bedroof tasseled
with cotes of cloud, with fountaining birds, with fire.
Such miracles in their sensual theatre,
vainly the lemur mewed, the locust whistled.
Truly, such miracles: one relenting breast
laid bare to drink his body through the palm;
their double flesh, quick as a wound with trust;
calendars drugged and smiling; and, in this womb,
the long thoughts of night: night comes at last,
and would it be on their side when it came?

ix
In diesem Wetter (Mahler)

Marram and bent-grass; lion-coloured gale
rampant among the hornets'-mist of dunes;
running northeast, a sea curled-axeheads: fail
if you can, faith, in this desolate womb of rains,
for it is reaving weather; and the streel
of desperate clouds, grey panic arch that spans
your aisle of absence, holds no rest at all.
Fail if you can. But while the hurt remains,
you have your proper food; and that will grow:
no shore too sandy for its brackish blood,
air too enormous for its knitted root.
What idle and exalted scrolls of blue,
arcadian sun, or sweet-lake-whisper, could
so breed endurance? And so vise the heart?

x
Preludi autunnali (Malipiero)

Eye-coloured sea, together we read your turning
sun-leaf in Kufic, and your minstrel sheets:
was there no other message than height and morning,
no flux to silver of your carol of lights?
This was the summer birth: no granite awaiting
memorials, beyond the twofold cradle,
no gilded letter tarnished? No room for doubting
your glitter of slow chisels was not idle?
Oh harbour-coloured eyes, what are you seeing
now the sung leaf is turned, or torn adrift,
the sistrum-light of water stilled and greying?
Bruise-blue of shadows; one small yacht beginning,
under the predatory wings, to lift
October sails, and run where the day is running.

xi
Petrushka (Stravinsky)

Till now, to others: when at last it happens
it hurts less finally than the dolls believe:
the hand that held the puppets falls and opens;
the puppets twist, and rise, and are alive.
But now they can no longer move together—
though (look) the strings are tangled. The freed limb
searches for muscles to replace its tether;
the muscles have no music ruling them.
But up, slack-sinewed; and a kind of bow
(no longer to a fellow) to the mirror;
then, out of habit, part of the old dance.
Look once around no-longer-home. And now
learn that your world had edges; and, with terror,
stare out across the waiting audience.

xii
Des pas sur la neige (Debussy)

Fold back the snow that haunts us: mantelpiece
and threshold, chimney (all the symbols lie)
are frozen; the wing-burning marigold eye
that lit our cradle will not will release.
Loose the loft summer that may not increase.
Loose the lascivious ivy's fingers, high
on the harnessed oak; loose our enclosing sky
to us, and in the sky its troubled fleece.
Granted, the snow bears footprints: something passed
and, out-of-sight beyond, gapes dead, or hides;
but that was gales ago, and is the last.
What moor from valley, tree from tree divides—
paled always—now is hugged into a waste
that nothing viable, falcon or fox, abides.

THAT SINGING MESH *

I planned for poems to be dressed in steel
and spider's-lace of harpstrings, that the flesh
(its nakedness unseen to pulse or feel)
dance under spectra in that singing mesh.

I grew my orchards with no living fruit:
poems were trees of wind-hung prisms, each
bejewelled like a grotto, the quick root
stalagmite-risen to stone plum or peach.

Time to shed filigree and crystal for
the naked body and the bitten drupe;
maze-music now, and rainbow-glass, no more,
but the high bird and the clear-polished loupe.

Now my faience and hippocras of rhyme
are shamed by peace of water and of delf;
the poet-archer tramples (it is time)
the poem-python that encoils itself.

This was the last root fertile, and this tree
shall bear its prisms too. But these are all:
and the last music in the sky shall be
a breaking string; and then the axes' fall.

NOTES

Insofar as any of these poems may be found at all "difficult", there are probably three linked causes; and much of the difficulty will disappear if warning of these is given.

First is the densely "Metaphysical" texture into which disparate and sometimes unexpected patterns of thought are plaited so as to make love-poems—which is what all these are, except the last, no matter how obliquely.

In the second place, these patterns of thought are built from symbols, metaphors, comparisons, glancing references, that have their origins in (for today) an unusually wide range of disciplines: most people no longer expect poetry to be learned. The difficulty here lies not in knowing technical terms (which can always be looked up) but in recognising them. For, everywhere, but especially in their use, there is a network of puns and Empsonian "ambiguities" one aspect of which will usually be erotic, and all aspects of which are usually structural parts of the poem.

Lastly, the punctuation is not always that recommended by text-books. Its intention, however, is that of all punctuation: to clarify the connexions between related images or ideas, and to preclude *unwanted* ambiguities.

A few specific "knots" are unravelled below.

Pages 14-15. Stage Directions and *Need-fires.* In these villanelles it will be found that each repetition of the refrains has a slightly different meaning. Note especially the various technical senses in which "fire" and "firing" are used.

15. Limits. ". . .a secretary's M". In at least one system of shorthand, M is represented by a convex curve. The imagery of the poem is concerned almost entirely with curves, some of which converge to (or close at) a definite limit, others of which diverge to infinity—aleph. In either case, they resemble some lovers.

16. Death by Water. St. Lawrence was reputedly grilled to death. Hugh Latimer was burned at the stake. The Venus's Flytrap is a carnivorous plant. Because of his adultery with Venus, Mars (Ares) was trapped in a net by her husband, Vulcan. The gate of horn is that through which true dreams issue; false come through that of ivroy. For Phlebas and the ocean, see *The Waste Land.* For Ophelia, the nunnery, and the river, see *Hamlet.* For Truth and the well that is her dwelling-place, see Democritus.

18-19. The Fugue of Poems and *Reading a Score.* Both poems pun extensively on musical terms (fugue, answer, unison, stop, suspension, wolf, *vox humana,* coupler, swell, mode, time, etc.) and on their non-technical and/or symbolically amorous meanings.

21ff. Triptychs. So called because there are three poems, written in *terza rima,* and concerned with various kinds of *three*—especially syllogisms. In Formal Logic, a syllogism is a three-stage piece of reasoning. There are many forms, technically "figures", each of which has several "moods", all having their own distinctive names. The simplest is in the form: All M is P; all S is M; therefore all S is P (as, for example: All cats are mammals; all lions are cats; therefore all lions are mammals). This mood of the first figure is called Barbara; and because of that name it has been treated in this group of poems *as a girl*—or as the Triple Goddess, one of whose aspects is Blodeuwedd. The names of other moods are prefixed to the second and third sections of the poem, in which they are treated (and illustrated) punningly.

Occam blade. The logical principle, "Occam's razor", that from every study or argument one must exclude inessentials. *Hampton patency.* "Hampton", from "Hampton Wick" is rhyming-slang for the penis. *Charvering* and *chivving* are petty-criminals' cant, originally Romany, for "copulating" and "knifing" respectively. *Nifë* (two syllables) is the Earth's hypothetical ferro-nickel core.

28ff. Diapason. I had originally planned a sequence of seven satirical treatments of the so-called "planets" of ancient cosmology, each poem incorporating references to the metals and jewels and other emblems and functions and superstitions associated with the planets and their appropriate gods or goddesses. Only three were completed. It may be noted that although Diana is not mentioned in the poem *Luna,* her virginity is suggested by references to the inert gases, the prime numbers, and rhymeless words. The rhyme-scheme of each poem is circular, to suggest the (traditional) planetary orbits.

Flower still where number itself extends. The number of prime numbers is infinite—as, probably, is also the number of transfinite numbers. *rare in your transits,* etc. Venus has the highest albedo (coefficient of reflected light) of all the true planets, but is only a dark spot when seen crossing the face of the sun—which happens only at intervals of 8 years, 235 years, and 243 years.

34. Last Supper. King Tereus violated Philomela, younger sister of his wife Procne. Procne cut up her son Itys, which means *willow,* and gave him to Tereus for supper. Eventually Philomela and Procne were turned into a nightingale and a swallow, respectively, and Tereus into a hoopoe. Looked at sardonically, the Last Supper foreshadowed a cannibal meal, and was a coven because there were thirteen present. The fish (like the lamb) is an emblem of Christ. For the Paschal Lamb, and blood on lintels, see *Exodus* 12, 2–8. Arachne was turned into a spider, in some species of which the female devours the male after copulation.

38ff. Pictorial Calendar. As the title suggests, each poem in this sequence describes a situation or a landscape associable with one of the twelve months. Equally, the "picture" of each sonnet symbolises a specific human mood or experience. The subtitles of the sonnet-stanzas are those of musical works. Sometimes the title is only verbally, or seasonally, appropriate to the matter; in other cases, the mood or content of the music is also relevant to those of the sonnet and/or of its month. The sequence as a whole depicts an unhappy love-story.
i. *Castor fiber* is the zoological name of the European beaver.
ii. The middle English quotation is from Chaucer's *Parlement of Foules*: It was believed that birds began to choose their mates on St. Valentine's Day. *Burke-lipped* combines "hare-lipped", the murderers Burke and Hare, and the orator Edmund Burke.
iii. A Throne is a member of the third Order of Angels.
iv. The quotations are from the folk-song *Bushes and Briars* itself—the tune of which is in the so-called Aeolian mode. *Imaginës* (four syllables) is the plural of *imago*, and is a complex pun upon psychological and entomological terms.
v. *Möbius tape.* A strip so twisted and joined that it is endless and only one-sided.

44. That Singing Mesh. *A breaking string,* etc. In *The Cherry Orchard*, Act Two, there comes from the sky the sound of a snapped harpstring—a symbol of approaching dissolution.

the poet-archer, etc. Apollo, god of poetry, who killed the great Serpent that lived in caves on Mount Parnassus.